VERSES WITH ANSWERS

What Kind of Person is Jesus?

Verses to Study
with Answers to Check
VOLUME 3

Dr. Noel Enete
Dr. Denise Enete

www.WaveStudyBible.com

Published by Wave Study Bible, Inc.
*www.***WaveStudyBible***.com*
Edition 1.1.0

The *4-Step* Bible study strategy was adapted from Anne Graham Lotz's *Living a Life that is Blessed*, Copyright 1995 by AnGel Ministries.

Cover by graphic artist and jazz musician Dorothy Collins Wineman, *http://www.dotcollins.com.*

ISBN 978-0-9791595-3-4

Table of Contents

Jesus is confident.
He does not fold
when the crowd
tells Him
He is wrong.

from Luke 8:43-48

1:
Introduction

"Would you please be my friend?" A kind but peculiar little woman in her fifties stood at our front door waiting for an answer. Her thick accent and tight bun caught me [D] off guard, but I knew I needed to say yes.

We had recently moved to a quaint little beach town in Southern California where everything was in walking distance, so we got in the habit of walking to church. Right after we moved in, I remember asking the Lord to allow me to "Feed His sheep." I knew He was answering my prayer.

Isabel explained she saw us walking to church, with Bible in hand, and wanted to be my friend so we could get together for Bible studies and fellowship. We arranged a time for our first meeting and I closed the door.

I remember telling the Lord "I meant other sheep Lord, sheep more like me." Good thing God is patient. Spending time with Isabel would become a highlight of my life. She had suffered and was healed from some of her many health issues and was a prayer warrior. She loved the Lord and He loved her. I was stretched in my times with her. She wanted to sing praise songs as part of our Bible study. At first I was self-conscious singing out loud where I could really be heard! But, Isabel sang with abandon and her voice was worse than mine, so I learned to just cut loose! I was her best friend and she cherished our weekly times together. The Lord used us in each other's lives.

I didn't think Isabel was what I was looking for when I asked God to let me feed His sheep, but He knew better. Many people make the same mistake with Jesus. They don't think He is what they are looking for—until they get to know Him. Then they find out He is exactly what they need.

First impressions can be misleading. The way you get beyond first impressions and really get to know somebody is by watching them in action.

There is no clearer way to see God in action than to watch Jesus in action because Jesus is God in the flesh. The way Jesus reacts to situations during His earthly ministry shows how God reacts to them. Some things bring Jesus joy, other things anger Him. At times He is moved to compassion and at other times He is moved to warn.

As you watch Jesus in action, notice what He values and ask yourself, "What kind of person values that?" Notice what moves Him to compassion and ask yourself, "What kind of person is touched by that situation?" Identify what angers Him and ask yourself, "What kind of person is angered by that kind of thing?" These questions help you understand Jesus' personality so you can trust Him the way you trust a true friend.

God does not present Himself to us as merely a collection of spiritual absolutes. He presents Himself as an infinite and divine person that is touched by our feelings and can be known like we come to know a friend. Do not miss the opportunity to know God.

Organization

This guide takes you through several gospel passages that show Jesus in action and lets you decide for yourself what kind of person He is.

The format of this guide encourages you to surface whatever you notice in the passages and respond to God accordingly. Then as you explore these passages, also be alert to notice what you can learn about what kind of person God is.

If you are not familiar with the *4 Step* method of studying the Bible, there is a section on page 7 that will explain what to write in the 4 panels associated with each passage.

A devotional commentary is also included after the passages that covers what you have just studied. This gives you something to compare your work against. The commentary also suggests a number of personality traits that can be learned about Jesus from the passages.

4-Step Bible Study Method

Following each passage in this guide are four panels that hold the results of our study of the passage. If you would like to print the 4 blank panels on page 10, you could write down the results of your study then compare them with ours. Our answers will help you see if you are generally on the right track.

1. Facts

In the *Facts* panel, make a list of the *Facts* you see in the passage. You don't have to list all the details. Just try and find the main points. You can use the same words as are in the passage. You will usually get somewhere around four to six *Facts*.

2. *Lessons*

In the *Lessons* panel, look over the list of facts and see what you can learn from the passage.

- Is there an example to follow?
- Is there a behavior to stop or start?
- Is there a comfort to accept?

Also, consider what you can learn about God from this passage? What does He value? What does He respond to? What pleases Him? You don't have to find a *Lesson* from every verse. Usually you will get one or two *Lessons* from a passage.

3. *Challenges*

In the *Challenges* panel, turn each *Lesson* you surfaced into a question that *Challenges* you. Listen for God to speak to you. He may not speak to you through every verse, but He will speak to you. You will generally get the same number of *Challenges* as *Lessons*.

4. *Response*

In the *Response* panel, consider what God is saying to you through this passage and decide how you will respond. Write out your *Response* as a two or three sentence prayer.

Be heartfelt and honest with God. If needed, put "training wheels" on your *Response:* "Lord help me want this thing You value." Better to be honest and ask for help, than promise behavior you are not ready to keep.

5. *Commentary*

Now that you are clear on what *you* see in the passage, we give you the *Commentary* panel where we describe what *we* see in the passage. If you find something helpful in this panel, add it to your current understanding.

In this step you are comparing your study against that of an authority. If you did not have our short *Commentary* you could consult other *Commentaries*, pastors, or trusted Bible teachers. If they differ from what you came up with, do not automatically discard your idea. Rather, look at both concepts and see which makes the most sense to *you* and adopt that as your new understanding.

Blank Panels to Print

For your convenience the following pages contain blank panels you could print and write on as you study the passages.

If you need a separate .PDF of these pages, you can download it from our web site *(http://wavestudybible.com/pages/goodies.html)*.

1. Facts

List what you see in the passage

2. Lessons

Write down what you learn from this passage

3. Challenges

Turn the lessons into questions that challenge you

4. Response

Listen to what God is saying to you and write out your response

Jesus responds
to small faith.

from Luke 8:40-42,49-56

2:
Verses

These passages take you through a study of Jesus in action. If you are unfamiliar with the *4-Step* method of studying the Bible, you will find a brief explanation on page 7.

For a more complete explanation, see our Bible study courses like Bible 101 *(cf. www.wavestudybible.com/wave101.html)* or our book, "How to Read the Bible So God Speaks to You" *(cf. www.wavestudybible.com/store.html or www.amazon.com).*

Passage 1—Luke 8:43-48

Luke 8:43 And a woman who had a hemorrhage for twelve years, and could not be healed by anyone,

Luke 8:44 came up behind Him and touched the fringe of His cloak, and immediately her hemorrhage stopped.

Luke 8:45 And Jesus said, "Who is the one who touched Me?" And while they were all denying it, Peter said, "Master, the people are crowding and pressing in on You."

Luke 8:46 But Jesus said, "Someone did touch Me, for I was aware that power had gone out of Me."

Luke 8:47 When the woman saw that she had not escaped notice, she came trembling and fell down before Him, and declared in the presence of all the people the reason why she had touched Him, and how she had been immediately healed.

Luke 8:48 And He said to her, "Daughter, your faith has made you well; go in peace." (NASB)

1. Facts

List what you see in the passage

A woman had a hemorrhage for 12 years.

She could not be healed by anyone.

She came up behind Jesus and touched the fringe of His cloak.

Immediately her hemorrhage stopped.

Jesus said, "Who touched Me?"

All denied it.

Peter told Him it was the crowd pressing in on Him.

Jesus said, "Someone did touch Me, for I was aware that power has gone out of Me."

The woman saw she had not escaped notice.

She came trembling.

She fell down before Him.

She said in the presence of all why she had touched Him and how she had been healed immediately.

Jesus said, "Daughter, your faith has made you well, go in peace."

2. Lessons

Write down what you learn from this passage

God can heal what men cannot heal.

Many people touched Jesus, but God recognizes our faith in any form.

Jesus wanted her to come forward and testify about her faith even though she was afraid. It was a way for her to meet Him personally and receive His comfort. God wants us to testify about our faith in Him. It is a way to connect with Him and encourage others.

The woman's testimony was a rebuke to the crowd who pressed on Him, but had no faith. We can be part of a church and never get any blessings from being close to Jesus if we have no faith.

Jesus "automatically" responded to faith. He did not interview her first to see if she was worthy of healing.

God's power flows toward our faith.

Sometimes it looks like God is wrong, but He is always right.

Jesus puts responsibility on us for our faith.

3. Challenges

Turn the lessons into questions that challenge you

Do I believe God can heal what is hopeless to man?

Do I have enough faith to draw God's power out?

Am I willing to come forward and testify about my faith even if I'm scared?

Do I think God responds to my faith or because I'm worthy?

If God is doing something that doesn't make sense, do I think He is wrong and try to correct Him, or wait and trust Him?

Am I taking responsibility for my faith?

4. Response

Listen to what God is saying to you and write out your response

Thank You Lord that You can heal so easily what is impossible for man. Thank You that Your power flows toward our faith. Please help me to increase my faith in You.

Commentary

Compare what you see with what an authority sees

The woman had been bleeding for 12 years. No one could stop the bleeding. They didn't have convenient bandages or pads in those days. She was probably anemic. She was considered unclean and could not partake in religious ceremonies. The problem had taken over her life and she was desperate for help. Desperate enough to seek out help from Jesus.

She had heard of His power to heal. She didn't dare demand a one-on-one session with Jesus, but thought just a touch of His cloak would be enough to heal her. Her heart quickened as she saw Him approach. The crowd was pressing in on Him, but this was her chance so she pushed in behind Him and touched the edge of His cloak. Her bleeding stopped at once.

Her euphoria was short-lived. Jesus knew that many people had touched Him, but her touch of faith was different. Jesus responded to a touch of faith. He had not touched her, she had touched Him. He wanted her to come forward and own her faith in Him, even if she was afraid. She came forward, afraid she was in trouble. She wasn't in trouble.

Jesus had automatically responded to her faith. He didn't interview her first to see if she was worthy of healing. He didn't rebuke her for touching Him while she was unclean. She had focused on Him as the answer. Jesus commended her for her faith in Him. He reassured her that she wasn't in trouble by telling her to go in peace.

But her testimony was a rebuke for the crowd, and us, who press on Him, but have no faith. It is possible to be part of a church and never get any blessings from being close to Jesus, because we have no faith.

Commentary

Compare what you see with what an authority sees

God's power flows toward our faith. That's why God says our faith is important. He responds to it. We are to take responsibility for our faith in Him. He does the rest. Am I taking responsibility for my faith?

What kind of person is Jesus?

- Jesus is persistent. The crowd denied touching Him. Peter said He was mistaken. Jesus persisted until the woman came forward.
- Jesus is powerful. Power flows out of Him.
- Jesus is confident. He does not fold when the crowd tells Him He is wrong.
- Jesus responds to faith in Him. Faith unlocks His power.
- Jesus wants to exercise His power, so He teaches the group (and us) that the woman's faith in Him, made her well.
- Jesus is kind. He saw the woman was afraid so He reassured her she was not in trouble by saying she could go in peace. Jesus is kind. She touched Him while she was unclean, but He overlooked that, and focused on her faith.

Passage 2—Luke 8:40-42, 49-56

Luke 8:40 And as Jesus returned, the people welcomed Him, for they had all been waiting for Him.

Luke 8:41 And there came a man named Jairus, and he was an official of the synagogue; and he fell at Jesus' feet, and [began] to implore Him to come to his house;

Luke 8:42 for he had an only daughter, about twelve years old, and she was dying. But as He went, the crowds were pressing against Him.

Luke 8:49 While He was still speaking, someone came from [the house of] the synagogue official, saying, "Your daughter has died; do not trouble the Teacher anymore."

Luke 8:50 But when Jesus heard [this,] He answered him, "Do not be afraid [any longer;] only believe, and she will be made well."

Luke 8:51 When He came to the house, He did not allow anyone to enter with Him, except Peter and John and James, and the girl's father and mother.

Luke 8:52 Now they were all weeping and lamenting for her; but He said, "Stop weeping, for she has not died, but is asleep."

Luke 8:53 And they [began] laughing at Him, knowing that she had died.

Luke 8:54 He, however, took her by the hand and called, saying, "Child, arise!"

Luke 8:55 And her spirit returned, and she got up immediately; and He gave orders for [something] to be given her to eat.

Luke 8:56 Her parents were amazed; but He instructed them to tell no one what had happened. (NASB)

1. Facts

List what you see in the passage

Jesus returned and the people welcomed Him.

They had been waiting for Him.

A ruler of the synagogue, named Jairus came.

He fell at Jesus' feet.

He pleaded with Jesus to come to his house.

His only daughter, about 12 years old, was dying.

The crowds were pressing around Jesus as he went.

While Jesus was still speaking someone from Jairus's house said, "Your daughter is dead; don't trouble the teacher any longer."

Jesus heard this and said to him, "Do not be afraid, just believe, and she will be healed."

Jesus did not let anyone go in the house except Peter, John, James and the child's parents.

Everyone was wailing and mourning for her.

Jesus said, "Stop your weeping for she has not died but is asleep."

They began laughing at Him, knowing she was dead.

Jesus took her by the hand saying, "Child arise."

Her spirit returned.

She got up immediately.

Jesus gave orders for her to be given something to eat.

Her parents were amazed.

Jesus instructed them to tell no one what had happened.

2. Lessons

Write down what you learn from this passage

Jesus responds to humility. Jairus was a ruler, yet fell at Jesus' feet with his request. We should approach Jesus humbly with our requests.

God helps us through trouble. He told Jairus what not to do (be afraid) and what to do (believe). That is what He wants us to do as we go through trouble.

God may tell us things we "know" are untrue, but we are wrong. We need to take God at His Word and not scoff.

God cares about our physical body. He knew the girl needed food, even though He had healed her. We need to take care of our body as well as our spirit.

3. Challenges

Turn the lessons into questions that challenge you

Do I approach Jesus humbly with my requests?

When I go through problems am I mostly afraid or am I believing?

Do I take God at His Word, and believe, or do I think I know best and scoff?

Do I realize God cares about my body and not just my spirit and soul?

4. Response

Listen to what God is saying to you and write out your response

Lord, please forgive me when I approach you with a caviler attitude instead of awe and reverence. Please help me to always have a sense of Who You are.

Commentary

Compare what you see with what an authority sees

When was the last time you fell to the floor with your request of God? Jairus fell at Jesus' feet with his request. Jesus responds to humility. He is willing to help us through our trouble when we turn to Him.

But, sometimes Jesus' advice seems wrong. Upon hearing his daughter was dead, Jesus told Jairus to not be afraid, but just believe and she would be healed. He said she was not dead, but asleep. The professional mourners, friends, neighbors and family "knew" she was dead. They chose to trust their own street smarts, rather than Jesus' Word. They laughed at, and ridiculed, Jesus. It must have been the professional mourners who laughed at Jesus, revealing their lack of true grief. The rest, who cared about the girl, might have let their fear and helplessness turn into anger. They bit the Hand that was feeding them so Jesus did not allow them in. He did not do His tender, loving miracle for dozens of unbelieving critics to watch.

Jesus gave Jairus the formula for working through problems: don't be afraid and just believe. Jairus did not have great faith. He thought Jesus needed to come to his home and touch her in order to heal his daughter. His friends advised him to leave Jesus when his daughter died, because they did not know He could raise the dead. But, Jairus's small faith was enough. Jesus took her gently by the hand and said, "Child arise." She got up immediately.

Color Jairus and his wife astonished. It would have been an even better experience for them if everyone had believed Jesus' word, instead of ridiculing Him. They probably felt ashamed of their behavior after He saved their daughter's life.

Commentary

Compare what you see with what an authority sees

We will be tempted to scoff and ridicule God when our problems seem insurmountable and He advises us to not be afraid, but just take Him at His Word. We have the chance to take God at His Word. It is a much better experience, from start to finish, if we choose to let go of our fear and take God at His Word—even if we have to go against our own street smarts. I don't want to feel ashamed of my behavior when I see Jesus. How about you?

What kind of person is Jesus?

- Jesus takes charge. He did not allow the unbelieving critics to witness the miracle. He told the parents to keep it a secret. He has His reasons.
- Jesus is reassuring. When Jairus hears his daughter is dead, Jesus immediately reassures him and gives him direction. He cared about his pain.
- Jesus is nurturing. He cared about the girl. He had just healed her, but wanted her to get the food her body needed. Jesus cares about us. He knows our needs. He wants us to believe that.
- Jesus responds to small faith. Jairus thought Jesus would need to touch his daughter in order to heal her. He did not have faith that Jesus could raise her from the dead.

Passage 3—Mark 2:1-12

Mark 2:1 When He had come back to Capernaum several days afterward, it was heard that He was at home.

Mark 2:2 And many were gathered together, so that there was no longer room, not even near the door; and He was speaking the word to them.

Mark 2:3 And they came, bringing to Him a paralytic, carried by four men.

Mark 2:4 Being unable to get to Him because of the crowd, they removed the roof above Him; and when they had dug an opening, they let down the pallet on which the paralytic was lying.

Mark 2:5 And Jesus seeing their faith said to the paralytic, "Son, your sins are forgiven."

Mark 2:6 But some of the scribes were sitting there and reasoning in their hearts,

Mark 2:7 "Why does this man speak that way? He is blaspheming; who can forgive sins but God alone?"

Mark 2:8 Immediately Jesus, aware in His spirit that they were reasoning that way within themselves, said to them, "Why are you reasoning about these things in your hearts?

Mark 2:9 "Which is easier, to say to the paralytic, 'Your sins are forgiven'; or to say, 'Get up, and pick up your pallet and walk'?

Mark 2:10 "But so that you may know that the Son of Man has authority on earth to forgive sins"--He said to the paralytic,

Mark 2:11 "I say to you, get up, pick up your pallet and go home."

Mark 2:12 And he got up and immediately picked up the pallet and went out in the sight of everyone, so that they were all amazed and were glorifying God, saying, "We have never seen anything like this." (NASB)

1. Facts

List what you see in the passage

Jesus returned to Capernaum.

After a few days the news spread that He was home.

So many people came to hear Jesus preach there was no room to get in.

Four men carried a paralytic.

They could not bring the paralytic in because of the crowd.

They removed the roof above Jesus.

They lowered the paralytic on the stretcher into the room.

When Jesus saw their faith He said to the paralytic, "Son, your sins are forgiven."

Certain scribes sitting there were thinking He was blaspheming because only God can forgive sins.

Immediately Jesus knew in His Spirit what they thought and asked them why they thought this.

Jesus said which is easier to say to the paralytic, "Your sins are forgiven" or say, "get up, pick up your pallet, and walk?"

Jesus told the paralytic, "Stand up, take your stretcher and go home."

He did this to show He had authority on earth to forgive sins.

Immediately the man stood up, took his stretcher and went out.

All were amazed and glorified God.

They had never seen anything like it.

2. Lessons

Write down what you learn from this passage

God loves it when we do what it takes to seek Him out.

Finding Jesus is a priority and way more important than personal property or appearances.

Being helpless did not keep the paralytic from recruiting the help he needed to see Jesus.

We are each responsible to do what it takes to be with Him.

Forgiveness of sins is a greater gift, and more important, than physical healing.

Jesus wants us to know He has authority to forgive sins. He responds to faith in Him.

God knows our thoughts and is willing to talk and reason with us about them.

3. Challenges

Turn the lessons into questions that challenge you

Do I do what it takes to seek Jesus out when I need Him?

Am I more worried about appearances and obstacles than spending time with Jesus when I need help?

Am I willing to recruit the help, or do what it takes to spend time with Jesus?

Do I value physical health more than forgiveness of sins?

Do I believe, and rest in, Jesus' ability to forgive my sins?

Do I think I am hiding my thoughts from Jesus, or am I willing to talk and reason with Him about them?

4. Response

Listen to what God is saying to you and write out your response

Lord, please help me to do what it takes to be with You. I need Your help. Please help me to accomplish all that you want me to, and not waste time making excuses.

Commentary

Compare what you see with what an authority sees

If you were paralyzed, would you be willing to recruit four men to help you get the help you needed? Would you also be willing to "make a scene" and bust up the meeting to get that help?

I can picture this paralytic rounding up the four men and instructing them to get him to Jesus. Hopes were high until they arrived and saw the entrance was blocked by swarms of people.

At this point the paralytic didn't lose his confidence and say, "Thanks anyway, it was a good try." No, this guy said, "Get me in there. Take off the roof!" He wasn't worried about personal property or how "desperate" he looked. He knew he needed help, and he knew Jesus could heal.

Jesus wasn't focused on the personal property either. He was focused on the group's faith in Him. Aren't you glad Jesus didn't reprimand them for taking the roof apart? What is fixing a roof compared with eternal forgiveness? He supported and rewarded their faith in front of everyone by forgiving the paralytic.

But, who forgives sin the scribes reasoned? They decided He must be blaspheming. Jesus was giving a huge clue that He was God, but they chose not to believe. Even though the scribes had not said anything out loud, Jesus read their mind (another clue) and asked them why they were so unbelieving.

In a generous gesture, Jesus continued by asking them which is easier to say, "Your sins are forgiven," or to say, "Get up, pick up your pallet and walk?" Then He healed the paralytic so that they would know He has authority on earth to forgive sins. They didn't deserve the demonstration, but Jesus gave them every chance to believe.

The paralytic had come thinking his physical condition was his greatest need. Jesus told him that forgiveness of sins was an even greater need than the need to walk. Jesus came for a spiritual ministry first. Healing was secondary. Sometimes we come to Jesus with the wrong priorities. But faith is what He enjoys the most.

What Kind of a Person is Jesus?

- Jesus enjoys when we do what it takes to be with Him, even if we have to be a bit radical to make it happen. He focuses on our faith and is not critical.
- Jesus is serious about the importance of forgiving sins. He is not focused on this temporary life and whether we can walk. He is focused on eternity and having us with Him.
- Jesus has authority and power to heal and forgive.
- Jesus is gracious to give extra evidence of His deity so we have every chance to believe.

Passage 4—Luke 19:1-10

Luke 19:1 He entered Jericho and was passing through.

Luke 19:2 And there was a man called by the name of Zaccheus; he was a chief tax collector and he was rich.

Luke 19:3 Zaccheus was trying to see who Jesus was, and was unable because of the crowd, for he was small in stature.

Luke 19:4 So he ran on ahead and climbed up into a sycamore tree in order to see Him, for He was about to pass through that way.

Luke 19:5 When Jesus came to the place, He looked up and said to him, "Zaccheus, hurry and come down, for today I must stay at your house."

Luke 19:6 And he hurried and came down and received Him gladly.

Luke 19:7 When they saw it, they all [began] to grumble, saying, "He has gone to be the guest of a man who is a sinner."

Luke 19:8 Zaccheus stopped and said to the Lord, "Behold, Lord, half of my possessions I will give to the poor, and if I have defrauded anyone of anything, I will give back four times as much."

Luke 19:9 And Jesus said to him, "Today salvation has come to this house, because he, too, is a son of Abraham.

Luke 19:10 "For the Son of Man has come to seek and to save that which was lost." (NASB)

1. Facts

List what you see in the passage

Jesus was passing through Jericho.

A rich tax collector named Zaccheus was there.

Zaccheus was small and unable to see Jesus because of the crowd.

He climbed a tree in order to see Jesus.

Jesus looked up and said, "Zaccheus, hurry and come down, for today I must stay at your house."

He hurried down and received Jesus gladly.

The onlookers grumbled that Jesus had gone to be a guest of a sinner.

Zaccheus stopped.

Zaccheus said, "Behold, Lord, half of my possessions I will give to the poor, and if I have defrauded anyone or anything, I will give back four times as much."

Jesus replied, "Today salvation has come to this house, because he, too, is a son of Abraham. For the Son of Man has come to seek and save that which was lost."

2. Lessons

Write down what you learn from this passage

God notices when we make extra effort to find Him. We should look for, and embrace, opportunities to be with Him.

God knows us and our name before we know Him.

Jesus did not shun Zaccheus even though he was a despised sinner who exploited people. Jesus won't shun us when we reach out to find Him. He came to save the lost.

It is never too late while we walk on earth to stop, repent of our sin, and make restitution.

3. Challenges

Turn the lessons into questions that challenge you

Am I making an extra effort to find God? Do I embrace opportunities to be with Him?

Am I confident He will notice?

Do I realize God knows me by name, even if I feel insignificant?

Do I think God shuns me if I sin?

Do I shun people when they sin?

Is there something I need to stop doing, repent and make restitution?

4. Response

Listen to what God is saying to you and write out your response

Lord, forgive me when I don't make the effort to find You in Your Word. You are there and I don't always do what it takes to see You and be with You. Thank You for being so compassionate and kind to sinners who seek You out.

Commentary

Compare what you see with what an authority sees

Jesus surprised everyone by suddenly calling out to a sinner in a tree who was seeking Him. Zaccheus was ready to change his life. He wanted to see Jesus, and did what it took to see Him—which in this case meant climbing a tree.

He did not expect Jesus to know him by name or to accept him so readily. But once he had Jesus' attention, Zaccheus announced the changes he wanted to make in his life. Jesus was pleased. Zaccheus was the kind of person Jesus had come to save—the lost who come to Him in repentance.

God notices when we make the extra effort to find Him. In that culture, men of Zaccheus's rank did not run. They did not climb trees. That was undignified. But Jesus loves a sinner who embraces and appreciates the opportunity to be with Him. This is the only time in scripture where Jesus invites Himself to be a guest in a home, and Zaccheus's heart was ready. He was joyful at the prospect of the visit. Jesus does not shun sinners who come to Him. This is why He came.

But proud "rule keepers" sometimes have a problem with extending forgiveness and grace to "known sinners." They were not looking on Zaccheus's heart like Jesus was. They were looking at his past sin, and wanted to keep him frozen there.

Just like Jonah didn't want to preach to the known sinners in Nineveh and the older brother didn't want his father to forgive his repentant prodigal brother, proud "rule keepers" can have ill will towards repentant "rule breakers."

The proud need to come to Jesus and repent of their pride and malice. Jesus doesn't want us to be rebellious. But He also doesn't want us to be self sufficient and proud. He wants all of us to come to Him in humble repentance.

What kind of person is Jesus?

- Jesus is focused on us.
- Jesus knows us by name.
- Jesus knows where we are.
- Jesus responds when we reach out to Him.
- Jesus does not shun sinners even though all sin is against Him.
- Jesus has compassion for sinners.
- Jesus responds to humility. Zaccheus ran and climbed a tree to see Him. He didn't care if he looked undignified. Jesus rewarded him by coming to his house.

Passage 5—Luke 17:11-19

Luke 17:11 While He was on the way to Jerusalem, He was passing between Samaria and Galilee.

Luke 17:12 As He entered a village, ten leprous men who stood at a distance met Him;

Luke 17:13 and they raised their voices, saying, "Jesus, Master, have mercy on us!"

Luke 17:14 When He saw them, He said to them, "Go and show yourselves to the priests." And as they were going, they were cleansed.

Luke 17:15 Now one of them, when he saw that he had been healed, turned back, glorifying God with a loud voice,

Luke 17:16 and he fell on his face at His feet, giving thanks to Him. And he was a Samaritan.

Luke 17:17 Then Jesus answered and said, "Were there not ten cleansed? But the nine--where are they?

Luke 17:18 "Was no one found who returned to give glory to God, except this foreigner?"

Luke 17:19 And He said to him, "Stand up and go; your faith has made you well." (NASB)

1. Facts

List what you see in the passage

Jesus was on His way to Jerusalem.

He passed between Samaria and Galilee.

Ten men with leprosy called from a distance, "Jesus, Master, have mercy on us."

When Jesus saw them He said, "Go show yourselves to the priests."

As they went along they were cleansed.

When one saw he was healed he turned back, praising God with a loud voice.

He fell with face on the ground at Jesus' feet and thanked Him.

He was a Samaritan.

Jesus asked, "Were not ten cleansed? Where are the other nine?"

Did only the foreigner turn back to give God glory?

Jesus told the man, "get up and go your way. Your faith has made you well."

2. Lessons

Write down what you learn from this passage

God answers our requests in unusual ways and if we don't trust Him and obey, we will miss the healing or blessing.

We need to be bold and ask God for what we need or want.

God responds to thankfulness and those who give Him glory.

God healed all ten lepers. He did not do it on a merit system. We do not merit His blessings. Our focus should be on Him, and giving Him glory, and not on ourselves and what we did to cause the blessing.

We need faith in Jesus to save us and make us whole.

3. Challenges

Turn the lessons into questions that challenge you

If I asked God for healing and He told me to go to show myself to the priests, would I obey and trust Him, or would I get irritated, because He wasn't healing me the way I expected?

Am I willing to be bold in my requests, regardless of how I look?

Am I thankful for all God gives me and willing to stop and fall at His feet and give Him glory?

Do I think I am meriting God's blessings? When something good happens, do I think it is a result of my good behavior?

Is my focus on God and giving Him glory, or on me and trying to earn His favor?

Is my faith firmly in Christ for salvation and making me whole?

4. Response

Listen to what God is saying to you and write out your response

Lord, please help me to be bold in my requests of You. Thank You for being so responsive—to those who ask. Thank You for healing all ten and not doing it by a merit system. Please help me to be forever thankful for Your great blessings and mercies.

Commentary

Compare what you see with what an authority sees

Jesus was on His way to Jerusalem. He hears 10 lepers shouting to Him from a distance. It would have been easy to ignore them. Just keep walking. Just keep walking. There are plenty of distractions and people to talk with. But, that is not Jesus. He listens to their request.

Then He does not tell them, "OK, you are healed." Instead He says, "Go and show yourselves to the priests." If they are humble and willing to do what He says, they will discover their healing as they go to the priests.

But what would have happened if they got irritated and said to one another, "He just blew us off. What good will showing ourselves to the priest be? We are unclean, the priest doesn't want to see us." Would they have been healed if they refused to trust and obey Jesus' Word? The passage doesn't say, but I'm inclined to believe their response of obedience was part of the healing deal. We can cut off God's blessings in our life when we dictate what form the blessings should take.

The lepers asked boldly. They raised their voices. They got His attention. But, they also asked respectfully.

I like Jesus' generous response. He healed them all. He did not use a merit system. "OK, I can heal 6 of you, but Sam, Pete, Joe and Barney have been too sinful to merit a healing." No, Jesus healed them all because no one merits His blessings. The lepers started out very well with boldness and with a focus on Jesus' ability to heal them, and with enough respect to follow His directions.

But, then the wheels on the wagon fall off a bit. They get what they wanted and are healed! So what is their first response? For the Samaritan, his first response is to turn back, fall at Jesus' feet and praise God with a loud voice. He doesn't have anything more important to do. But, the others have better things to do. Their focus is no longer on God, they have what they want.

Jesus wasn't done giving to the thankful Samaritan. He told him his faith had made him whole. The others might have been healed, but he was saved as well.

God loves to give to us. But if this causes us to not need Him anymore, we cut off His blessings because we can't handle them. Turning back and falling at His feet and praising Him with a loud voice is one of the sweetest moments we will share with God. Too bad nine of them missed it.

What Kind of Person is Jesus?

- Jesus is willing to be interrupted.
- Jesus is responsive. He was walking to Jerusalem, but willing to respond to requests along the way.
- Jesus is very generous. He healed all the men when they asked and then saved the Samaritan when He saw his faith.
- Jesus is not an egomaniac. After He saw the Samaritan's faith, He told him to get up and go his way. Jesus did not need the Samaritan bowing to Him all day.

Passage 6—Luke 19:28-35

Luke 19:28 After He had said these things, He was going on ahead, going up to Jerusalem.

Luke 19:29 When He approached Bethphage and Bethany, near the mount that is called Olivet, He sent two of the disciples,

Luke 19:30 saying, "Go into the village ahead of [you;] there, as you enter, you will find a colt tied on which no one yet has ever sat; untie it and bring it [here.]

Luke 19:31 "If anyone asks you, 'Why are you untying it?' you shall say, 'The Lord has need of it.'"

Luke 19:32 So those who were sent went away and found it just as He had told them.

Luke 19:33 As they were untying the colt, its owners said to them, "Why are you untying the colt?"

Luke 19:34 They said, "The Lord has need of it."

Luke 19:35 They brought it to Jesus, and they threw their coats on the colt and put Jesus [on it.] (NASB)

1. Facts

List what you see in the passage

Jesus was going to Jerusalem.

When He got to the Mt. of Olives He sent two the of disciples to the next village.

He told them to find a colt that was tied there and had never been ridden and bring it.

He said if anyone asks why you are untying it say, "The Lord needs it."

They found the colt exactly as He had told them.

As they were untying the colt the owner asked, "Why are you untying the colt?"

They replied, "The Lord needs it."

They brought it to Jesus.

They threw their cloaks on the colt.

Jesus got on it.

2. Lessons

Write down what you learn from this passage

Jesus can see places without being there. He can work His plan using people who can't see ahead, but trust and obey His instructions.

Jesus knows the future. He knew what the response of the owner of the colt would be. Jesus can use us when we cooperate with what "the Lord needs." We should use our resources for what "the Lord needs."

Jesus can control animals. The unridden colt let Him ride him. Jesus is Master over His creation. We are just custodians of His animal Kingdom. We should honor Him as we do our job of managing His creation.

Jesus' ways are not our ways. He did not have the disciples seek out the owner of the colt to get his permission first. Jesus owns the colt. He was "commanding" the colt's use and knew the owner would cooperate with His need.

The disciples gave what they had to honor Jesus. They threw their cloaks on the colt. They probably would have preferred to give a horse draw chariot fit for a king, but they didn't have the means for that. They gave what they had. That was what Jesus wanted.

3. Challenges

Turn the lessons into questions that challenge you

Am I willing to trust and obey God's instructions even if the plan seems risky?

Do I have an open hand with the resources God has given me? Am I willing to use them for what "the Lord needs?"

Am I honoring God as Master over His creation and doing my part to be a good custodian of His animal kingdom?

Do I realize God owns everything? Am I cooperating with His kingdom needs?

Am I giving God what I have, or do I think I should wait til I have more to give?

4. Response

Listen to what God is saying to you and write out your response

Lord, thank You that You can see places without being there. Thank You for having a plan and using ordinary people who can't see ahead. Please help me to trust and obey Your instructions. I want to be part of Your plan. I want to use the resources You have loaned to me to meet whatever needs You have.

Commentary

Compare what you see with what an authority sees

Jesus was a low-maintenance man. He didn't have His own place to live, His own money, or His own mode of transportation. He did not demand much for Himself. So when He asked to use the colt we know it was important.

Jesus could have commandeered a four horse chariot. That would have been way more impressive than a colt. But Jesus wanted the colt, and not just any colt. It had to be a colt that had never been ridden. Most animals have to be broken in before they are rideable. But since Jesus is Master over His creation, the colt was subject to Him and cooperated.

Jesus' ways are not our ways. He did not have the disciples seek out the owner of the colt to get his permission first. Jesus owned the colt. He was "commanding" the colt's use and knew the owner would cooperate with His need. Jesus knows the future. He knew what the response of the owner of the colt would be.

Jesus can use us when we cooperate with what "the Lord needs." Am I willing to use my resources for what "the Lord needs" or do I think I don't have much of value for the Lord?

The disciples didn't have much either. But, they gave what they had. They gave their coats—a humble gift but rich in worship. I'm sure it was a gift Jesus loved. If I wait until I have something impressive to give to God, I don't understand the heart of God.

Commentary

Compare what you see with what an authority sees

What kind of person is Jesus?

- Jesus is specific about what He wants. He asked for a colt that had never been ridden.
- Jesus did not require much for Himself. He was not focused on making Himself comfortable. He was focused on doing His Father's will.
- Jesus is powerful and knows the future. He knew what the owner of the colts response would be.
- Jesus is powerful and is Master and Owner of His creation. An unridden colt cooperated for Him.

Passage 7—John 20:10-17

John 20:10 So the disciples went away again to their own homes.

John 20:11 But Mary was standing outside the tomb weeping; and so, as she wept, she stooped and looked into the tomb;

John 20:12 and she saw two angels in white sitting, one at the head and one at the feet, where the body of Jesus had been lying.

John 20:13 And they said to her, "Woman, why are you weeping?" She said to them, "Because they have taken away my Lord, and I do not know where they have laid Him."

John 20:14 When she had said this, she turned around and saw Jesus standing [there,] and did not know that it was Jesus.

John 20:15 Jesus said to her, "Woman, why are you weeping? Whom are you seeking?" Supposing Him to be the gardener, she said to Him, "Sir, if you have carried Him away, tell me where you have laid Him, and I will take Him away."

John 20:16 Jesus said to her, "Mary!" She turned and said to Him in Hebrew, "Rabboni!" (which means, Teacher).

John 20:17 Jesus said to her, "Stop clinging to Me, for I have not yet ascended to the Father; but go to My brethren and say to them, 'I ascend to My Father and your Father, and My God and your God.'" (NASB)

1. Facts

List what you see in the passage

The disciples went to their homes.

Mary stood outside the tomb crying.

While she cried, she bent down and looked inside the tomb.

She saw two angels in white sitting where Jesus' body had been lying.

One was at the head and one at the feet.

They asked Mary why she was crying.

Mary replied "They have taken my Lord away, and I do not know where they have put Him."

She turned around and saw Jesus standing there, but did not recognize Him.

Jesus said, "Woman why are you crying? Who are you looking for?"

She thought He was a gardener.

She said, "Sir if you have carried Him away, tell me where you have put Him and I will take Him."

Jesus said, "Mary."

She turned and said, "Rabboni" which means Teacher.

Jesus said, "Do not touch Me, for I have not yet ascended to My Father. Go to My brothers and tell them, 'I am ascending to My Father and your Father, to My God and your God.'"

2. Lessons

Write down what you learn from this passage

For those who look for Jesus, and linger when they can't find Him, He will come to them.

God cares about our feelings and asks us to express them to Him as a way to stir our faith.

Jesus' appearance is not always recognizable, but we will recognize His voice. His children recognize the power, love and majesty of His voice.

Jesus came so that His Father and God could become our Father and God.

3. Challenges

Turn the lessons into questions that challenge you

Am I willing to seek Jesus and linger when I don't immediately find Him, or do I just "go home"?

Do I believe that God cares about my feelings and wants me to express them to Him?

Do I realize that if I get to know Jesus I will recognize Him by His personality instead of just by appearance?

Do I appreciate how Jesus came so that His Father and God could become my Father and God?

4. Response

Listen to what God is saying to you and write out your response

Lord, thank You that You come to those who diligently seek You. Please forgive me for getting impatient at times and just "going home". Thank You for allowing me know You. Please help me recognize You by Your personality and not just by Your appearance.

Commentary

Compare what you see with what an authority sees

The angels and Jesus cared that Mary was crying. They both asked her to explain her tears even though they knew why she was crying. They were trying to wake up her faith. That was tender.

They could have just been exasperated. How many times did Jesus tell them He would die and rise again? Jesus could have said, "Don't cry dummy, it's Me." But He saw her grief and let her say something about it before He oriented her to the news.

If Mary and the disciples had taken in Jesus' teaching about rising on the third day, they should have been excited to find the body missing, not tearful.

But Jesus is patient and kind. He rewarded Mary for lingering and for trying to figure out how to find Him. She was half right—looking for a dead body—and He still rewarded her efforts. But it would have been better if she was looking for His risen body! God is willing to meet us where we are, as we make an effort to find Him.

Mary did not immediately recognize Jesus' appearance. The disciples would also not recognize Him on the beach. They did not expect to see Jesus risen from the dead, and unbelief is blind. When we aren't looking for a miracle, it is easy to miss when one happens. Mary was focused on her grief.

But Mary and the disciples knew Jesus. She recognized His loving tone and power when He said her name. We might not recognize Jesus' appearance, but His children will recognize His voice as they spend time with Him. His voice is different than other thoughts we may hear in our head.

Commentary

Compare what you see with what an authority sees

His voice has authority and confidence. It comes out of "no where." We don't think it up by ourselves. *"My sheep hear (recognize) My voice, and I know them, and they follow Me." (John 10:27)*

What kind of a person is Jesus?

- He is wildly generous. He died so that His Father could become our Father and His God could become our God. He calls us brothers.
- Jesus is tender. He asks us to express our sadness to Him, even when we are mistaken.
- Jesus is patient. He did not get exasperated when Mary was crying instead of being excited.
- Jesus is recognized by His power and love. They define His personality.

Passage 8—Luke 22:14-23

Luke 22:14 When the hour had come, He reclined [at the table,] and the apostles with Him.

Luke 22:15 And He said to them, "I have earnestly desired to eat this Passover with you before I suffer;

Luke 22:16 for I say to you, I shall never again eat it until it is fulfilled in the kingdom of God."

Luke 22:17 And when He had taken a cup [and] given thanks, He said, "Take this and share it among yourselves;

Luke 22:18 for I say to you, I will not drink of the fruit of the vine from now on until the kingdom of God comes."

Luke 22:19 And when He had taken [some] bread [and] given thanks, He broke it and gave it to them, saying, "This is My body which is given for you; do this in remembrance of Me."

Luke 22:20 And in the same way [He took] the cup after they had eaten, saying, "This cup which is poured out for you is the new covenant in My blood.

Luke 22:21 "But behold, the hand of the one betraying Me is with Mine on the table.

Luke 22:22 "For indeed, the Son of Man is going as it has been determined; but woe to that man by whom He is betrayed!"

Luke 22:23 And they began to discuss among themselves which one of them it might be who was going to do this thing. (NASB)

1. Facts

List what you see in the passage

When it was time Jesus sat down with the twelve apostles.

Jesus earnestly desired to eat the Passover with them before He suffered.

Jesus would not eat the Passover again until it is fulfilled in the kingdom of God.

He took a cup and gave thanks.

He instructed them to take it and divide it among themselves.

He said He would not drink the fruit of the vine until the kingdom of God comes.

He took bread and gave thanks.

He broke it and gave it to them.

He said, "This is My body which is given for you; do this in remembrance of Me."

In the same way He took the cup after they had eaten.

He said, "This cup which is poured out for you is the new covenant in My blood."

Jesus said the hand of the one betraying Him was sitting with Him at the table.

Jesus said the Son of Man's path has been determined.

But, woe to the man who betrays Him.

The disciples began to inquire among themselves which one would betray Him.

2. Lessons

Write down what you learn from this passage

God has an appointed time for how His plan unfolds. He does not do things haphazardly.

Jesus' path was predetermined. A betrayer or the evil one could not thwart His mission. God has also predetermined the good works we will walk in if we cooperate with His will.

Jesus gave thanks. He was aware and thankful of God the Father's provision. We should also be giving thanks for God's provision for us.

Jesus gave His body for us. He wants us to remember this by sharing communion together.

Jesus is willing to die in order to make a new covenant with us. He wants to be with us.

3. Challenges

Turn the lessons into questions that challenge you

Am I trusting God's timeline, or fretting?

Am I walking in the good works God has predetermined for me? Am I cooperating with His will?

Am I giving thanks to God for His provision for me?

Am I remembering Christ's sacrifice by sharing communion with other believers on a regular basis?

Am I living like I am in a new covenant with God? Do I believe He wants to be with me?

4. Response

Listen to what God is saying to you and write out your response

Lord, thank You that You have a plan and an appointed time for how Your plan will unfold. Thank You that You are in control and not haphazard or disorganized. Please help me to trust You completely and not fret when things aren't happening as fast as I want.

Commentary

Compare what you see with what an authority sees

God never needs to rush. When the hour had come, Jesus reclined at the table. He was willing to wait for that hour. Jesus' path was predetermined and He was carrying it out. There was no need to rush. No betrayer or evil one could thwart His mission. God had prepared the good works He was to walk in and Jesus cooperated.

Funny thing, God has also prepared the good works we are to walk in if we cooperate with His will. The evil one is still trying to thwart God's plan by inciting our desire for other things. Judas sold out for money. What tempts us to turn aside and betray Jesus? If we get frustrated because God is not rushing His plan, we will be more vulnerable for the temptation to betray Him for something else.

Jesus had previously hinted to His disciples that one would betray Him, but now He speaks openly about it. This is probably more for Judas's sake. Jesus had earlier greeted Judas with a kiss and washed his feet *(John 13),* but now He was giving him an opportunity to repent. Jesus did not openly identify him as the betrayer, but protected him until the end.

When we are facing a time of suffering, we need to do as Jesus did. Give thanks. He was aware and thankful for God-the-Father's provision, even though He would suffer greatly and be betrayed. He was willing to give His body for us and wants us to regularly remember with other believers His sacrifice.

We look back at what He did for us on the cross, and we look forward to His coming again. This helps us give thanks and keep our suffering in perspective. He wanted to be with us enough to die for us.

Commentary

Compare what you see with what an authority sees

Jesus showed His love by sharing this meal with His disciples. He could have been preoccupied with His own impending suffering, but He saw beyond the agony to the glory and crown. We can be grateful that Jesus is working His plan, at just the right time.

What kind of a person is Jesus?

- Jesus is thoughtful. He said His betrayer was with Him at the table. He was warning Judas of the consequences of his betrayal. Jesus might have stirred up intrigue by not directly naming Judas, but this is a kinder, less confrontational way of warning Judas of the consequences of the path he is planning.
- Jesus has poise. He never rushes around. He is doing His Father's will and carrying out the plan as was predetermined for Him.
- Jesus cares deeply about His disciples. He said He earnestly wanted to eat the Passover with them before He suffered. He had a fervent desire to prepare them for what was coming. He was not just focused on His upcoming suffering. He was passionate about His time with His disciples and how His death the next day would fulfill the symbolism of the Passover meal.
- Jesus is thankful. He was aware of God the Father's provision and said so.

Passage 9—John 4:7-15, 25-26

John 4:7 There came a woman of Samaria to draw water. Jesus said to her, "Give Me a drink."

John 4:8 For His disciples had gone away into the city to buy food.

John 4:9 Therefore the Samaritan woman said to Him, "How is it that You, being a Jew, ask me for a drink since I am a Samaritan woman?" (For Jews have no dealings with Samaritans.)

John 4:10 Jesus answered and said to her, "If you knew the gift of God, and who it is who says to you, 'Give Me a drink,' you would have asked Him, and He would have given you living water."

John 4:11 She said to Him, "Sir, You have nothing to draw with and the well is deep; where then do You get that living water?

John 4:12 "You are not greater than our father Jacob, are You, who gave us the well, and drank of it himself and his sons and his cattle?"

John 4:13 Jesus answered and said to her, "Everyone who drinks of this water will thirst again;

John 4:14 but whoever drinks of the water that I will give him shall never thirst; but the water that I will give him will become in him a well of water springing up to eternal life."

John 4:15 The woman said to Him, "Sir, give me this water, so I will not be thirsty nor come all the way here to draw."

John 4:25 The woman said to Him, "I know that Messiah is coming (He who is called Christ); when that One comes, He will declare all things to us."

John 4:26 Jesus said to her, "I who speak to you am [He.]" (NASB)

1. Facts

List what you see in the passage

A Samaritan woman came to the well to draw water.

Jesus said to her, "Give Me a drink."

His disciples had gone to buy food.

The Samaritan woman asked why He was speaking to her since the Jews shunned the Samaritans.

Jesus said, "If you knew the gift of God and Who it is Who says to you, 'Give Me a drink,' you would have asked Him, and He would have given you living water."

She said, "Sir, You have nothing to draw with and the well is deep; where then do You get the living water?"

"You are not greater than our father Jacob are You? He gave us the well and used it himself."

Jesus said, "Everyone who drinks this water will thirst again. Whoever drinks of the water I give, will never thirst because it becomes a well springing up to eternal life."

The woman said, "Sir, give me this water so I won't be thirsty and have to come to the well to draw."

The woman said, "I know that the Messiah Who is called Christ is coming."

"When that One comes, He will tell us everything."

Jesus said, "I Who speak to you am He."

2. Lessons

Write down what you learn from this passage

God initiates conversations with unlikely "undeserving" sinners and asks for their help. He is no respecter of persons and can use anyone.

We are all undeserving and God asks for our help. He asks us to help the widow and the orphan and make disciples. He asks us to help Him but He is really helping us.

We don't have to become "better" before God offers Himself to us.

God is not bound by cultural sins and idiosyncrasies. He loves everyone, Samaritans and Jews.

Jesus tries to get us to be eternally minded. We are focused on earthly water and He continues to point to forgiveness and eternal life as being more important.

Jesus clearly identifies Himself as the Messiah to those who seek Him.

3. Challenges

Turn the lessons into questions that challenge you

Am I willing to initiate a conversation with someone about Jesus' gift of eternal life?

Am I a respecter of people? Am I only willing to talk to those like myself?

Do I realize that by giving to others God helps me?

Do I think I need to clean up my act before I can meet with God?

Am I bound by cultural sins? If culture says supporting abortion and homosexuality are right do I stay quiet and go along with that?

Am I only focused on earthly concerns or am I heavenly-minded?

Do I see how clear Jesus was with His identity when the woman was open and seeking the truth? Am I that clear about Christ's identity with those who are open to finding Him?

4. Response

Listen to what God is saying to you and write out your response

Lord, thank You for being willing to use, talk to, and save, undeserving sinners. Thank You that You are no respecter of persons and You are willing to enlist the help of sinners. Please help me to be heavenly minded and not so focused on earthly concerns.

Commentary

Compare what you see with what an authority sees

Would you ever think of asking someone with shady moral character for help? That is what Jesus did. It was probably a rare occurrence for this woman to be asked to join in and help someone else! She was probably not even respected in her own Samaritan community. Disrespected people start to feel invisible. That could be why she came alone to draw water. Better to not feel the avoidance from the others in her community.

So the idea that a Jewish man would not only speak to her, but ask for her help, boggled her mind! It was a show of respect for her as a person. She surely started out thinking Jesus was confused, not realizing she was a Samaritan. But Jesus knew all about her. He asked her for help, but He was really there to help her.

There were three routes Jesus could have taken to get to His destination of Cana of Galilee. Even though the most direct route was through Samaria, the Jews didn't take that route because of their hatred for the Samaritan people. But Jesus took the route through Samaria. He wasn't bound by Jewish cultural sins. He came to help her, which would allow her to help many others.

Jesus gets right to the point. He offers her God's "living water"—a much better deal than the earthly water He requested from her. She starts out practical. How can He give her "living water" without a bucket? He appeals to her curiosity. There was something about Jesus, so she keeps probing. "Are You greater than Jacob?" Jesus doesn't answer that, but keeps talking about the "living water." She was focused on earthly thirst and the chore of drawing water. Jesus was focused on eternal life and quenching spiritual thirst.

Commentary

Compare what you see with what an authority sees

It is interesting that she decides she wants the "living water" so she won't have to come to the well anymore—wrong reason. But when she expresses her faith in the coming Messiah Who will come and tell her everything, Jesus seals the deal and clearly identifies Himself to her.

Just think about that for a moment. Jesus clearly reveals Himself as Messiah to this disrespected Samaritan woman. We don't have to become "better" before He offers Himself to us. God works with us where we are. In this chapter Jesus ministers to a variety of people: a sinful Samaritan woman, His own disciples, the many Samaritans who believed Him, and a nobleman and his household. What did they all have in common? They all believed in Him. For those who are humble enough to be open to Him and open to the truth, He offers Himself and His "living water," freely.

What Kind of Person is Jesus?

- Jesus is not affected by peer pressure. Men did not speak to unknown women. Jews did not speak to Samaritans. Jesus did what was right, even if it caused Him trouble and misunderstanding.
- Jesus is no respecter of persons. He initiates conversations with "undeserving" sinners.
- Jesus is willing to ask for help from the least of us.
- Jesus is clear about His identity with those who are open and seeking the truth.

Jesus
is willing to be
interrupted.

from Luke 17:11-19

3:
Appendix

About the Authors

Dr. Noel Enete

Noel has a Bachelors from Baptist Bible College, a Th.M. from Dallas Theological Seminary in original language exegesis and a Doctor of Education specializing in Internet-based training systems. He has taught Bible and Theology for Dallas Bible College and has authored the *Wave Study Bible®* app for those with an iPhone, iPad, or iPod Touch.

Dr. Denise Enete

Denise has a Bachelors from Baptist Bible College and Masters course work at Dallas Theological Seminary. She also has a Masters and Doctor of Psychology and has had a private clinical psychology practice. Her specialty is integrating biblical truth with principles of good mental health. She has written a monthly column for a local paper on mental health topics and published a story in *Chicken Soup for the Bride's Soul.* They have been married since 1972 and have four adult children.

Contact

If you have suggestions or simply have benefited from this book, feel free to drop the authors an e-mail at the address below. Unfortunately, they will probably not be able to reply, but they would love to hear from you.

noel.enete@wavestudybible.com
denise.enete@wavestudybible.com

*(their last name is pronounced eee **NET**)*

CPSIA information can be obtained at www.ICGtesting.com
Printed in the USA
BVOW01s2148030614

355347BV00001B/2/P